First Facts

Faceless, Spineless, and Brainless Ocean Animals

SEA URCHINS

by Jody S. Rake

Consultant:
Dr. Deborah Donovan
Professor, Biology Department and Science Education Group
Western Washington University
Bellingham, Washington

CAPSTONE PRESS
a capstone imprint

First Facts are published by Capstone Press,
1710 Roe Crest Drive, North Mankato, Minnesota 56003
www.mycapstone.com

Library of Congress Cataloging-in-Publication Data
Cataloging-in-Publication Data is on file with the Library of Congress.
Names: Rake, Jody Sullivan, author.
Title: Sea urchins / by Jody S. Rake.
Description: North Mankato, Minnesota : Capstone Press, [2017] | Series:
   First facts. Faceless, spineless, and brainless ocean animals | Audience:
   Ages 7-9.? | Audience: K to grade 3.? | Includes bibliographical
   references and index.
Identifiers: LCCN 2015051440| ISBN 9781515721505 (eBook PDF) | ISBN 9781515721420
(hardcover) | ISBN
   9781515721468 (pbk.)
Subjects: LCSH: Sea urchins—Juvenile literature.
Classification: LCC QL384.E2 R25 2017 | DDC 593.9/5—dc23
LC record available at http://lccn.loc.gov/2015051440

Editorial Credits
Abby Colich, editor; Bobbie Nuytten, designer; Kelly Garvin, media researcher; Steve Walker, production specialist

Photo Credits
Minden Pictures: Bruno Guenard/Biosphoto, 17, Peter Verhoog, 7, Sue Daly, 9; Newscom/Image Quest 3-D/NHPA/Photoshot, 19; Shutterstock: Andrey Luzhanskiy, 5, Dudarev Mikhail, 20, LauraD, 10, 14, littlesam, 11, Mandy Madness, 13, Vilainecrevette, cover, 1, 15, 21

Artistic Elements
Shutterstock: Artishok, Vikasuh

Printed and bound in China

PO007692RRDF16

Table of Contents

No Backbones

Can you think of an animal without a backbone? Many sea animals do not have a backbone. Animals without backbones are **invertebrates**. Sea urchins are invertebrates. They have no faces or brains either. Other body parts help them move and find food.

Fact! Sea urchins were once called sea hedgehogs.

invertebrate—an animal without a backbone

Urchins Everywhere

Sea urchins live in oceans all over the world. Some like the cold, offshore water. Others live in warm waters close to land. Sea urchins that live near the shore tend to be loners. Sea urchins that live beyond the shore gather in **hordes**.

All Shapes and Sizes

There are about 700 **species** of sea urchins. They come in every color. Most are just one bright color. Others are many colors. Sea urchins are usually 2.3 to 4.6 inches (6 to 12 centimeters) wide. Most are the size of a tomato.

horde—a large group
species—a group of creatures that are
capable of reproducing with one another

Porcupines of the Sea

Sea urchins look like little porcupines. Their hard, shell-like bodies are covered with spines. The hard body beneath the spines is called the **test**. At the bottom of the test is the mouth. Inside the mouth are five hard teeth.

Sea urchins slowly creep around on tube feet. Tube feet look like noodles. They work like suction cups. They hold tight and then let go.

Fact! Sea urchins' teeth are very strong. They can **bore** into solid rock!

spine

tooth

tube foot

test—a sea urchin's body
bore—to drill

Super Spines

Sharp spines help protect sea urchins from **predators**. The spines are usually less than 1 inch (2.5 cm) long. Spines on larger urchins can reach 8 inches (20 cm) long. Some sea urchin spines are as thick as pencils. Others are needle-thin.

Fact! The spines aren't stuck in place. A **joint** holds each spine to the body. The joint lets the spine swivel around.

predator—an animal that hunts another animal for food
joint—a place where two parts meet

Undersea Grazers

Most sea urchins scoop up food bits with their mouths as they crawl. Some urchins scrape algae off rocks. Others munch away on seaweed. Sometimes bits of food fall on them from above. Some sea urchins can use their spines to move this food into their mouth.

Fact! Some sea urchins make poison in their spines. When touched, the spine shoots out the poison.

A Ring of Nerves

Sea urchins don't have brains. Instead they have a system of **nerves**. The nerves run around the inside of their bodies like a ring. They help the spines and tube feet move.

Fact! A sand dollar is a type of sea urchin that is flattened.

nerve—a thin strand in the body that carries messages

Don't Mind the Spines

Spines don't keep sea urchins safe from all predators. Sea otters carefully handle the spiny creature. They crack the urchin open on a rock. Then they eat the soft parts inside. Triggerfish use their mouths to yank out a sea urchin's spines. Then they chow down.

Sea Urchins and People

People also eat sea urchins. In Japan sea urchin eggs are a **delicacy**. The eggs sell for as much as $200 for 1 pound (0.45 kg)! Overfishing has caused the decline of many species. Some sea urchins are **endangered**.

wolf eel eating a sea urchin

delicacy—a food that is considered rare

endangered—at risk of dying out

Sea Urchin Life Cycle

Male and female sea urchins release **reproductive cells**. The cells meet in the water. Then they grow into **larvae**. The tiny larvae drift. Once they grow large enough, they sink to the seafloor. Soon they grow into young sea urchins.

reproductive cell—a male or female cell needed to make offspring

larva—a stage of development between egg and adult

Fact! The larvae drift around for weeks. But once they reach the seafloor, the change is lightning fast. They can develop their hard, spiny bodies in about one hour!

larva

Amazing But True!

Sea urchins have no eyes, but they still seem to sense light. Sea urchins will move away from bright lights. How? Scientists believe sea urchins have special cells on their tube feet. The cells can sense light.

Sea Urchin Facts

Where it lives: oceans worldwide

Habitat: found in all ocean habitats

Size: body 2.3 to 4.6 inches
(6 to 12 cm) long;
spines 0.5 to 8 inches
(1.3 to 20 cm) long

Diet: algae, bits of leftover food

Predators: sea otters, triggerfish,
wolf eels, large sea stars

Life span: 30 years or more,
sometimes up to
200 years

Status: Some species are overfished
and at risk of dying out.
Other species are stable.

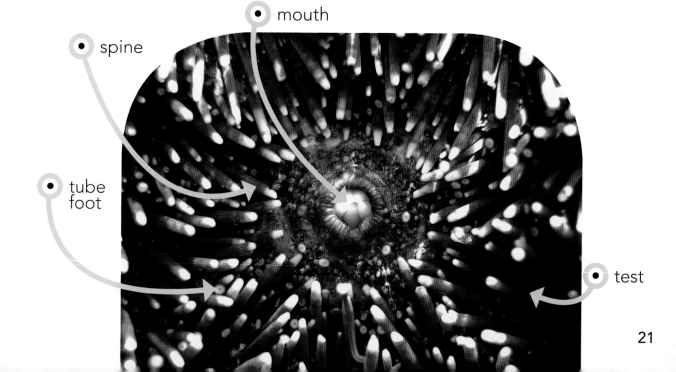

spine

mouth

tube
foot

test

Glossary

bore (BOR)—to drill

delicacy (DEL-uh-kuh-see)—a food that is considered rare

endangered (in-DAYN-juhrd)—at risk of dying out

horde (HOARD)—a large group

invertebrate (in-VUR-tuh-bruht)—an animal without a backbone

joint (JOYNT)—a place where two parts meet

larva (LAR-vuh)—a stage of development between egg and adult

nerve (NURV)—a thin strand in the body that carries messages

predator (PRED-uh-tur)—an animal that hunts another animal for food

reproductive cell (ree-pruh-DUCK-tiv SELL)—a male or female cell needed to make offspring

species (SPEE-sheez)—a group of creatures that are capable of reproducing with one another

test (TEST)—a sea urchin's body

Read More

Magby, Meryl. *Sea Urchins*. Under the Sea. New York: PowerKids Press, 2013.

Rajczak, Michael. *Sea Urchins*. Things That Sting. New York: Gareth Stevens Publishing, 2016.

Rose, Simon. *Sea Urchins*. Ocean Life. New York: AV2 by Weigl, 2012.

Internet Sites

FactHound offers a safe, fun way to find Internet sites related to this book. All of the sites on FactHound have been researched by our staff.

Here's all you do:

Visit *www.facthound.com*

Type in this code: 9781515721420

Check out projects, games and lots more at
www.capstonekids.com

Critical Thinking Using the Common Core

1. Name a sea urchin body part and describe how it helps the animal survive. (Key Idea and Details)

2. Reread the sidebar on page 6. Then find two different pictures of sea urchins in the book. Describe how they are different. Then describe what likenesses they have that make them both sea urchins. (Craft and Structure)

3. What if the sea urchin had a face with eyes? How might its life be different? (Integration of Knowledge and Ideas)

Index